THE *Magna Book* OF

~

IMPRESSIONISTS

~

AN INSPIRED COLLECTION
OF THE IMPRESSIONISTS'
BEST-LOVED WORKS

DEDICATION
For my parents

Editor: Fleur Robertson
Editorial Assistance: Nicola Dent, Laura Potts, Jillian Stewart
Original Design Concept: Peter Bridgewater
Design: Jill Coote
Picture Research: Leora Kahn
Director of Production: Gerald Hughes
Production: Ruth Arthur, Sally Connolly, Neil Randles
Typesetting: Julie Smith

Jacket: *Le Moulin de la Galette* (detail)
Pierre-Auguste Renoir, Musée d'Orsay, Paris

CLB 3147
This 1993 edition published by Magna Books
Magna Road, Wigston, Leicester LE18 4ZH
© 1993 Colour Library Books Ltd.
Godalming, Surrey, England.
Printed and bound in Singapore.
All rights reserved.

ISBN 1-85422-403-4

THE *Magna Book* OF

IMPRESSIONISTS

JULIET RODWAY

MAGNA
BOOKS

In troduction

Today, when the French Impressionists are so popular, it is hard for us to understand why their paintings were greeted with such outrage when first exhibited in 1874. Their colourful, radiant images of everyday life seem as fresh and as true to our experiences now as the day they were painted. At the time, however, most of the Impressionists received nothing but scorn for their efforts. Monet, Pissarro and Manet did not achieve real success until late in their careers; Cézanne had his first one-man show in 1895, when he was fifty-six, and Van Gogh only sold one painting in his entire life!

The first Impressionist exhibition opened on April 15, 1874 at the photographer Nadar's studio on the Boulevard des Capucines, Paris. The chief contributors were Monet, Degas, Renoir, Morisot, Sisley, Pissarro and Cézanne. Manet, sometimes called the leader of the group – much to his annoyance – did not participate, preferring to submit his paintings to the Salon, the usual route for an artist seeking fame and fortune. The Salon was an enormous exhibition held annually at the Palais de l'Industrie on the Champs Elysées in Paris. Thousands of entries were received every year and work was often poorly displayed, crammed into every available corner. Once a painting had been selected by the Salon's jury, the artist had a good chance of gaining recognition and, subsequently, commissions. By far the most important category of painting accepted was the 'history' painting. This was normally a large-scale work based on a subject drawn from the classics, mythology, Christianity or ancient history, and was considered the highest form of art. To the young artists emerging under Napoleon III's Second Empire, this style of painting seemed academic and hackneyed.

The Impressionists wanted to paint subjects that were entirely representative of modern life – everyday scenes of people dancing, eating or bathing, of performers at the theatre or riders at the racetrack; they covered the whole spectrum of human activity. The influx of Japanese prints into Europe and the development of photography encouraged them to introduce daring new viewpoints and to lighten their colours. Landscape was also of prime importance. Monet, Sisley and Pissarro, in particular, strove to capture the immediacy of the moment. They painted outdoors, directly from nature, filling their canvases with atmosphere, light and colour. As they needed to work quickly, they developed a sketch-like technique which involved using small, often unmixed, brightly coloured dabs of paint. Compared to the more sombre, carefully modelled and highly finished paintings of the Salon, the difference was startling.

Not surprisingly, the Impressionists found their work continually rejected by the Salon. In reaction, they were prompted to organize their own exhibition. This move attracted much interest, partly because, apart from the Salon, there were only a handful of exhibition venues in Paris. Private art-dealers were a rarity; Paul Durand-Ruel was one of the few willing to help the Impressionists. Unfortunately, the critics and the public alike could not understand the paintings. Finding the subject matter inappropriate and the technique inexplicable, they were vitriolic in their condemnation.

From 1874 to 1886 there were eight Impressionist exhibitions; only Pissarro, the father-figure of the group, took part in all eight. By the time the Impressionists had dispersed, a new generation of artists had emerged, led by Gauguin, Seurat and Lautrec, who, with their roots in Impressionism, were to push back the boundaries of art still further. Despite the clashes of personality and the differences in their styles, the Impressionists were united by a single passionate objective – to depict the world around them in all its modernity. In doing so, they evolved an exciting and forceful new art form.

Bar at the Folies-Bergère

Manet was already in the latter stages of a terminal illness when he painted this, his final masterpiece. He recreated the scene in his studio, using a model placed behind a table. The unusual position of the barmaid's reflection in the mirror – moved from its logical place behind her to the far right – and that of the man – whose back should be visible to the viewer – has given rise to much discussion. At the very least, the positioning avoids interrupting the barmaid's hypnotic gaze, giving the painting great power. Shortly after this work's completion, Manet was awarded the Legion of Honour. Although it was the official recognition he had always craved, he remained bitter, feeling success had come too late. He died the following year, aged fifty-one.

1882
38" x 51"
Oil on canvas
Courtauld Institute, London

10

Impression, Sunrise

This famous painting gave the Impressionist movement its name when it was reviewed in 1874. Monet's title was chosen by critics to poke fun at the painter's sketch-like technique – one journalist claimed that wallpaper was better finished than *Impression, Sunrise*, inventing the term 'Impressionism' as an insult. Yet, despite the ridicule, Monet succeeded in selling the work for 800 francs and the name 'Impressionist' became accepted.

Painted in Le Havre, probably in one morning, this priceless canvas – a fine example of Monet's attempts to capture a single moment in time – was stolen from the Musée Marmottan in 1985. Fortunately, it was recovered five years later.

1872
20" x 25"
Oil on canvas
Musée Marmottan, Paris

Wild Poppies

In 1871, Monet moved to the small town of Argenteuil on the River Seine, just northwest of Paris, with his first wife Camille and their young son, Jean. Thanks to the patronage of the art-dealer Paul Durand-Ruel, Monet's finances improved temporarily, and as a result the family's early years spent at Argenteuil were particularly happy and productive. Here the artist was to create some of his early masterpieces, among them this world-renowned painting of Camille and Jean enjoying a warm and peaceful summer's day. Poppy fields featured time and again in Monet's work, but rarely with such freshness.

1873
20" x 26"
Oil on canvas
Musée d'Orsay, Paris

La Gare St-Lazare

Of the numerous paintings by Monet of St-Lazare station in Paris, this is one of the most famous. According to Renoir, the poverty-stricken painter had donned his best suit and grandly announced himself to the station master as Monsieur Monet, the Painter, inferring by his manner that he was an important personage from the art world. The official, knowing no different, consented to clear the platforms of passengers, halt the trains and stoke the engines to produce steam for Monet to paint. The results conclusively proved wrong those critics who had claimed that fog and steam were not fit subjects for art.

1877
30" x 41"
Oil on canvas
Musée d'Orsay, Paris

Waterlilies, Harmony in Green

In Monet's great 'series' works of the 1890s he chose to concentrate on a single subject, painting it repeatedly, often from the same angle, but at different times of the day and in various weathers. Of these, his waterlily paintings are the most renowned and numerous.

At his home in Giverny, Monet diverted the River Epte – to the horror of the locals, who feared he would pollute it with his exotic plants – to create a perfect water garden, the centrepiece of which was a simple Japanese footbridge. Despite his failing eyesight, he spent his final years in this garden, painting the play of light on water that had fascinated him all his life.

1899
35" x 37"
Oil on canvas
Musée d'Orsay, Paris

Poplars near Moret-sur-Loing

This evocative painting of a walk lined with poplars on a fresh, windswept day was executed in the town of Moret-sur-Loing, near the Forest of Fontainebleau, where Sisley settled in 1883. Of all the Impressionists, Sisley was perhaps the most consistent in style. He was chiefly a landscape painter, living most of his life in great poverty for the sake of his art. Rarely did he sell his works and when he did it was for very little money. Regarded as a minor painter all his life, he died destitute and in great pain. Ironically, shortly after his death his talent was recognized and the value of his work rose sharply. Today he is considered one of the finest Impressionists.

1890
26" x 32"
Oil on canvas
Musée d'Orsay, Paris

Le Moulin de la Galette

It was once said of Renoir that he never produced a sad painting and indeed his undoubted *joie-de-vivre* is brilliantly reflected in this lively impression of a Parisian open-air dance hall.

Renoir worked on the spot, daily carrying the huge canvas to and fro from his studio on the nearby Rue Cortot. He deliberately softened the outlines of the figures until they almost merge into one another, and added splashes of colour to suggest the light filtering through the trees. With hardly a sharp edge anywhere, the painting has a remarkable sense of movement, perfectly capturing the spirit of this cheerful occasion.

1876
52" x 69"
Oil on canvas
Musée d'Orsay, Paris

Madame Charpentier

This almost regal portrait probably flattered its sitter a little, for it was in Renoir's nature to be considerate towards his subject and this particular person was very influential. Madame Charpentier was renowned for her literary salons, which were attended by celebrities from the world of French politics, literature and the arts. Mingling in this high society, far removed from his own working-class origins, led to several profitable commissions for Renoir. With this painting and a larger portrait of Madame Charpentier and her children, Renoir had great success at the Salon exhibition of 1879. For all his care not to offend, however, Renoir never compromised his artistic integrity.

1876-1877
18" x 15"
Oil on canvas
Musée d'Orsay, Paris

Luncheon of the Boating Party

This masterpiece marks the high point of Renoir's Impressionist career. It is a brilliant portrayal of a relaxed summer gathering of his friends and is one of his last works based on the camaraderie of his early life.

After painting this, Renoir felt he had achieved all he could with Impressionism and began to look in new directions. It also marked the end of his bachelorhood, for the pleasingly plump woman holding the dog is Aline Charigot, his future wife. Indeed, love is in the air everywhere in this picture – virtually everyone in the painting appears to be flirting with someone else, either through conversation or by making eye contact. Perhaps, therefore, it is fitting that Renoir's beloved should only look adoringly at her dog.

1881
51" x 68"
Oil on canvas
Phillips Collection, Washington

The Cradle

Morisot was the first woman to join the Impressionists. The sister-in-law of Edouard Manet, she encouraged him to try painting in the open air and to introduce a lighter range of colours to his work. It was rumoured that she once loved him, certainly she was his most talented pupil, drawing most of her inspiration and subject matter from her family life and immediate surroundings.

This charming portrait shows her sister Edma gazing lovingly at her first child, Jeanne, seen through a veil of voile. Morisot was to participate in all the Impressionist exhibitions, except one in 1879 when she gave birth to her daughter.

1873
22" x 18"
Oil on canvas
Musée d'Orsay, Paris

Racehorses in Front of the Stands

A lifelong admirer of the thoroughbred's clean lines, Degas studied racehorses at Haras-du-Pin in Normandy in the 1860s and later observed them on the racetracks of Paris and New Orleans. He preferred to paint the tense moments before a race, rather than the race itself.

Although the painting is carefully constructed, Degas gives it a casual air by placing the two foreground horses with their backs to the viewer and by cutting the right horse's head by the picture frame. The result is a glimpse of contemporary life – like a snapshot. Although Degas sketched from life, he finished the composition in his studio, believing that his memory would reveal the essence of the subject far more effectively than simply copying nature.

c. 1868
18" x 24"
Oil on canvas
Musée d'Orsay, Paris

L'Absinthe

This sober portrait of two of Degas' friends – the actress Ellen Andrée and the painter Marcellin Desboutin – was originally entitled *At the Café*, but was renamed *L'Absinthe* when it was exhibited in London in 1893. The public, unaccustomed to seeing such realistic depictions of daily life in oils, rather than in illustrations or prints, did not understand the painting and, finding it shocking, felt the need to invest it with a moral. In polite society of the time it was held to be shameful for a woman to drink publicly, and absinthe – a cheap form of alcohol – had a sleazy reputation. For this dejected character to be drinking, apparently alone and forgotten in a café, suggested immorality to the nineteenth-century viewer.

Perhaps it is likelier, however, that Degas was simply showing the lonelier side of café life.

1876
36" x 27"
Oil on canvas
Musée d'Orsay, Paris

L'Étoile

In this picture of a ballet dancer, Degas beautifully captures the magic of the performance, while at the same time showing its artificial nature. The figures waiting in the wings would not be visible to the audience; thus Degas' unusual viewpoint emphasizes the make-believe world of ballet.

Degas' father, a wealthy banker, held weekly concerts at his home, instilling in the young artist a lifelong love of music, theatre and ballet. Nearly half of Degas' later work consists of ballet and theatre paintings, many in pastel – a medium he liked for its versatility and ease of use. Here, the wings of the stage are drawn in broad, rough strokes, contrasting with the smooth open stage and the delicate touches on the dancer's costume.

c. 1876
24" x 14"
Pastel on paper
Musée d'Orsay, Paris

Woman Drying her Neck

By the time Degas drew this pastel he was in his sixties and almost blind, but his interest in physical movement remained as keen as ever.

Known to be a cynical, bad-tempered bachelor, Degas' pastels of women at their toilet, such as this one, earned him the unfair reputation of being a woman-hater. The critics called these works obscene because they did not conform to the traditional view of women as objects of idealized beauty. They were outraged that Degas drew his models in ordinary, everyday poses, rather than in the noble, erotic or highly stylized ones beloved of classical art. Yet, though Degas' women were drawn with a cool, detached eye, to modern eyes they are nonetheless beautiful.

c. 1895
25" x 26"
Pastel on paper
Musée d'Orsay, Paris

Apples and Oranges

Still life was the ideal subject for Cézanne's analytical approach to art as it enabled him to experiment without interruption. He spent days arranging the objects to his satisfaction and often took so long over a picture that he had to replace his real flowers, long since dead, with artificial ones. In this rich, colourful painting, he contrasts the roundness of the fruit with the more angular folds of the drapery.

Cézanne was completely dedicated to his art; he lived like a recluse, even, on occasions, keeping his family at a distance. By 1886 he was financially secure, his father having left him two million francs, but not even the temptations of this great fortune swayed him from his course.

1895-1900
29" x 37"
Oil on canvas
Musée d'Orsay, Paris

The Card Players

This painting is usually considered the best of Cézanne's five versions of *The Card Players*. A slow, methodical worker and a hard taskmaster, the artist required his models – usually friends – to keep still for hours on end. A portrait of the dealer, Vollard, is said to have needed over one hundred sittings before Cézanne abandoned it!

Cezanne stressed the composition and structure of a scene to a greater degree than other Impressionists. Unlike them, he wished to reveal the essence of an object by reducing it to its basic geometric form. He considered that this approach would give a scene a sense of greater permanence, and create an art more durable, than one based on the impressions of a fleeting moment.

1890-1892
18" x 23"
Oil on canvas
Musée d'Orsay, Paris

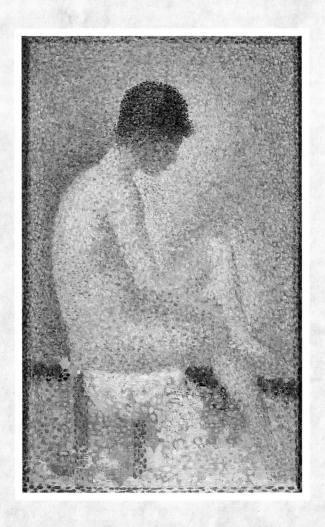

$\mathcal{N}ude\ in\ \mathcal{P}rofile$

This is one of three preliminary studies for Seurat's large-scale painting, *The Models*. It demonstrates his theory of Optical Mixture, whereby thousands of dots of unmixed colour, set side by side and viewed from the correct distance, blend in the viewer's eye to create the painting's specific forms and colours.

This highly analytical approach to art had a mixed reception with the Impressionists. Monet, whose style of painting was much more spontaneous, scorned Seurat and his followers. Renoir and Sisley would have nothing to do with them; only Pissarro defended them.

Sadly, Seurat's career was tragically curtailed when he died of diphtheria at thirty-one.

1877
10" x 6"
Oil on canvas
Musée d'Orsay, Paris

Chestnut Trees at Louveciennes

This is one of only forty paintings Pissarro saved from his home in Louveciennes, west of Paris, after it had been occupied by the Prussians during the Franco-Prussian War and converted into a slaughterhouse. Hundreds of his paintings were destroyed by the soldiers who used them as duckboards to cover the muddy ground.

From 1869 Pissarro rapidly developed his Impressionist style. In *Chestnut Trees* he used looser brushstrokes and brighter colours than before to convey the feeling of a cold winter's day. Monet, Renoir and Sisley also worked in Louveciennes around 1870 and there are distinct similarities in the approach of each artist. Monet and Sisley, in particular, shared Pissarro's fascination with the effects of light on the snow.

1870
16" x 21"
Oil on canvas
Musée d'Orsay, Paris

44

Woman in a Close

In 1884 Pissarro rented a large house in Eragny, near Paris, converting the barn into a studio. Here he continued to paint the rural landscapes that were his trademark, but now he concentrated more on the human figures in them, particularly peasants at work. Another change occurred in 1885 when he met the artist Georges Seurat.

Seurat's theories of Optical Mixture and his way of using only dots of colour to paint captivated Pissarro for a while. In *Woman in a Close, Springtime at Eragny,* (to give the painting its full title), Pissarro has used this style, but in a noticeably less rigid manner than Seurat. The result is this lively, even glowing, impression of a crisp and sunny spring morning.

1887
22" x 26"
Oil on canvas
Musée d'Orsay, Paris

Van Gogh's Room in Arles

In 1888, two years after his meeting with the Impressionists and his introduction to Japanese prints, Van Gogh moved to Arles in the south of France in search of southern light and the exotic colours of Japan.

He rented the Yellow House, furnishing it sparsely with money provided by his generous and ever-supportive brother, Theo. He spent much time and effort trying to make the house as welcoming as possible, installing gas lighting and decorating the guest bedroom with his paintings. When all was ready, he invited Gauguin to join him and, shortly before the artist's arrival, painted this view of his bedroom. He wanted the picture to suggest, through its simple form and colours, utter restfulness. For a while in the Yellow House, Van Gogh felt he had come home.

1889
23" x 29"
Oil on canvas
Musée d'Orsay, Paris

The Siesta

This work was painted at Saint-Rémy asylum, where Van Gogh had been admitted as a voluntary patient after a seizure and the self-mutilation of part of his ear. It is a copy of one of Jean-Francois Millet's paintings from a series *The Four Hours of the Day*.

Millet's images of peasant life had long influenced Van Gogh and here he has successfully translated them into his own personal style. As usual with this artist, the work was painted fast, using dark outlines and bright, thickly applied colours. Yet, despite his vigorous brushwork, Van Gogh has retained a sense of tranquillity here.

1889-1890
29" x 36"
Oil on canvas
Musée d'Orsay, Paris

50

Dr Paul Gachet

In 1889, Van Gogh moved to Auvers, where Dr Gachet, a homeopathic physician and lover of art, looked after him. They quickly became great friends, Vincent sensing in Gachet a fellow sufferer of the nervous disorders he had long endured.

This portrait, completed at Gachet's request, probably reflects Van Gogh's character as much as his sitter's. Certainly Gachet's kind, forgiving expression of gentle melancholy gives some clue as to why Vincent found him such sympathetic company. Nevertheless, for all his care, the doctor could not stave off the feelings that were to drive Van Gogh to despair and suicide just over a month after finishing this work.

1890
27" x 23"
Oil on canvas
Musée d'Orsay, Paris

The Alycamps

This is a view of the Alycamps in Arles in the south of France – an avenue lined with poplar trees and Roman tombs, bordered by a canal. The building in the distance is the ruined chapel of Saint-Honorat. It was painted during Gauguin's tempestuous stay with Van Gogh – the two frequently argued – at a time when he was just emerging from the influence of the Impressionists. The short, almost staccato, brushstrokes are reminiscent of Van Gogh's technique, if somewhat more restrained. It is unlikely that it was painted on the spot as the relationship between the chapel and the canal is different in reality.

1888
36" x 29"
Oil on canvas
Musée d'Orsay, Paris

Arearea

In 1891 Gauguin left France on his first visit to the South Sea island of Tahiti. He had already separated from his wife and children in order to pursue his artistic career; now he rejected Western civilization in his search for happiness and a freer, purer lifestyle.

In Tahiti, he lived among the natives, adopting one girl, Tehura, as his 'wife'. He loved to paint the Tahitian women and was often inspired by their folk tales – in this painting (the title is Tahitian for 'Joyousness') we are shown these women in a moment of relaxation. Gauguin developed an almost naive style of painting, characterized by large flat areas of vivid colour surrounded by strong outlines. His work almost always reflected the tropical climate of Tahiti – its rich hues and inspiring, dazzling light.

1892
21" x 30"
Oil on canvas
Musée d'Orsay, Paris

The Clown Cha-U-Kao

As a child, Toulouse-Lautrec had the misfortune to break both his legs; they failed to heal properly and he was left stunted and crippled. By way of compensation, he concentrated on his art.

Although born into the French aristocracy, Toulouse-Lautrec loved to paint Parisian low-life, particularly the performers from the bars, nightclubs and music halls, such as Cha-U-Kao, the female clown from the Moulin Rouge. Her unusual name was derived from the French word for the high kick in the cancan – *chahut*. Like Degas, Toulouse-Lautrec was a superb draughtsman. In a few rapid strokes, using paint thinned with turpentine, he has captured the essence of this woman's character.

1895
25" x 19"
Oil on cardboard
Musée d'Orsay, Paris

Acknowledgements

The publishers would like to thank the following
for permission to reproduce:–

Art Resource, New York, for the last page, title
page and pp. 10-11, 12-13, 14-15, 18, 35, 37;

The Bridgeman Art Library, London,
for the back flap and pp. 26-27;

Copyright, Paris, for the jacket and pp. 16-17,
22-23, 25, 28, 30-31, 32, 38-39, 41, 42, 44-45,
46-47, 48-49, 50-51, 52, 55, 56-57, 59;

Musée Massena for pp. 20-21;

the Musée d'Orsay, Paris, and
the Musée Marmottan, Paris.

Title page and facing page:
After the Bath by Edward Degas
Musée d'Orsay, Paris